T0109138

METAL
COLORING BOOK
CATS

ALEXANDRA CROCKETT
Illustrations by CHUCK GONZALES

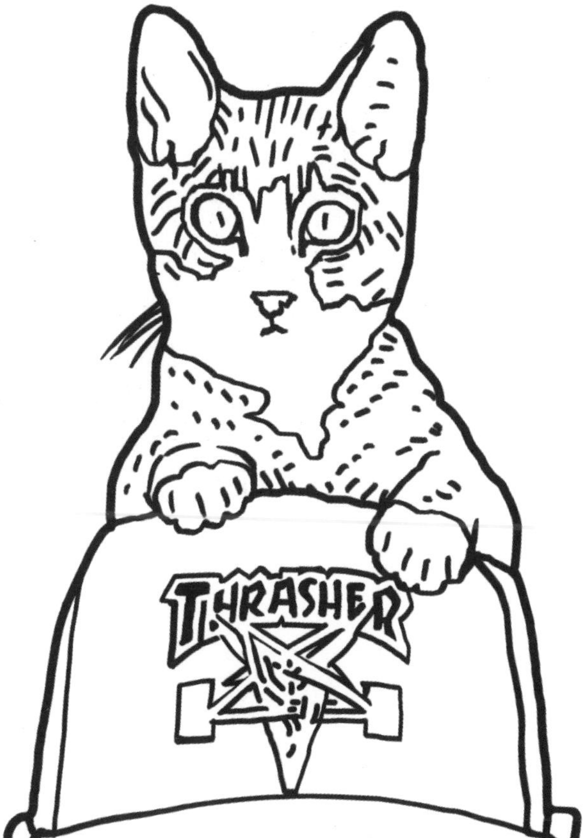

pH powerHouse Books Brooklyn, NY

Die By

SAT FEB 5TH
behemoth
LED
ZEPPELIN
STAIRWAY TO HEAVEN

AMON AMARTH

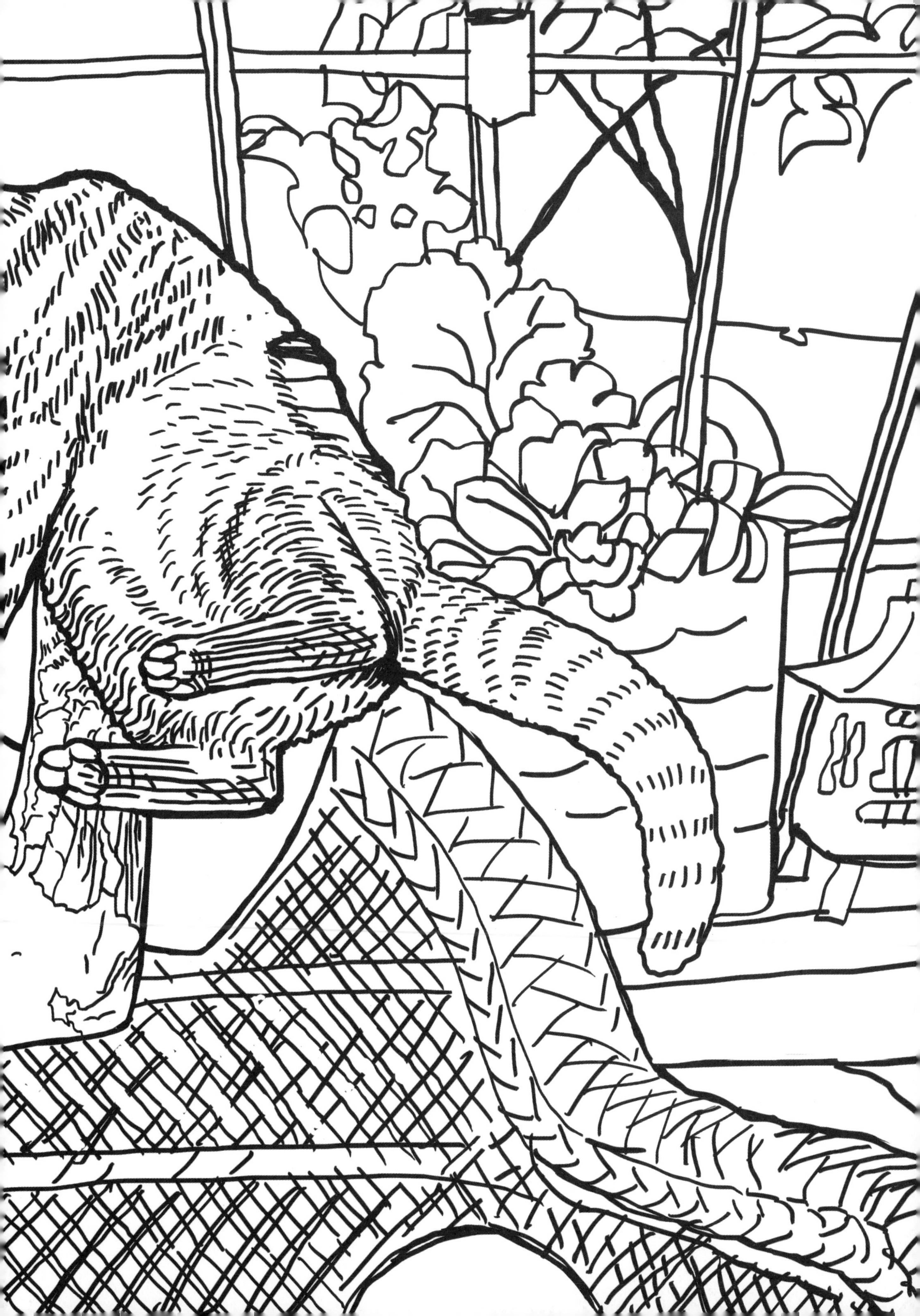

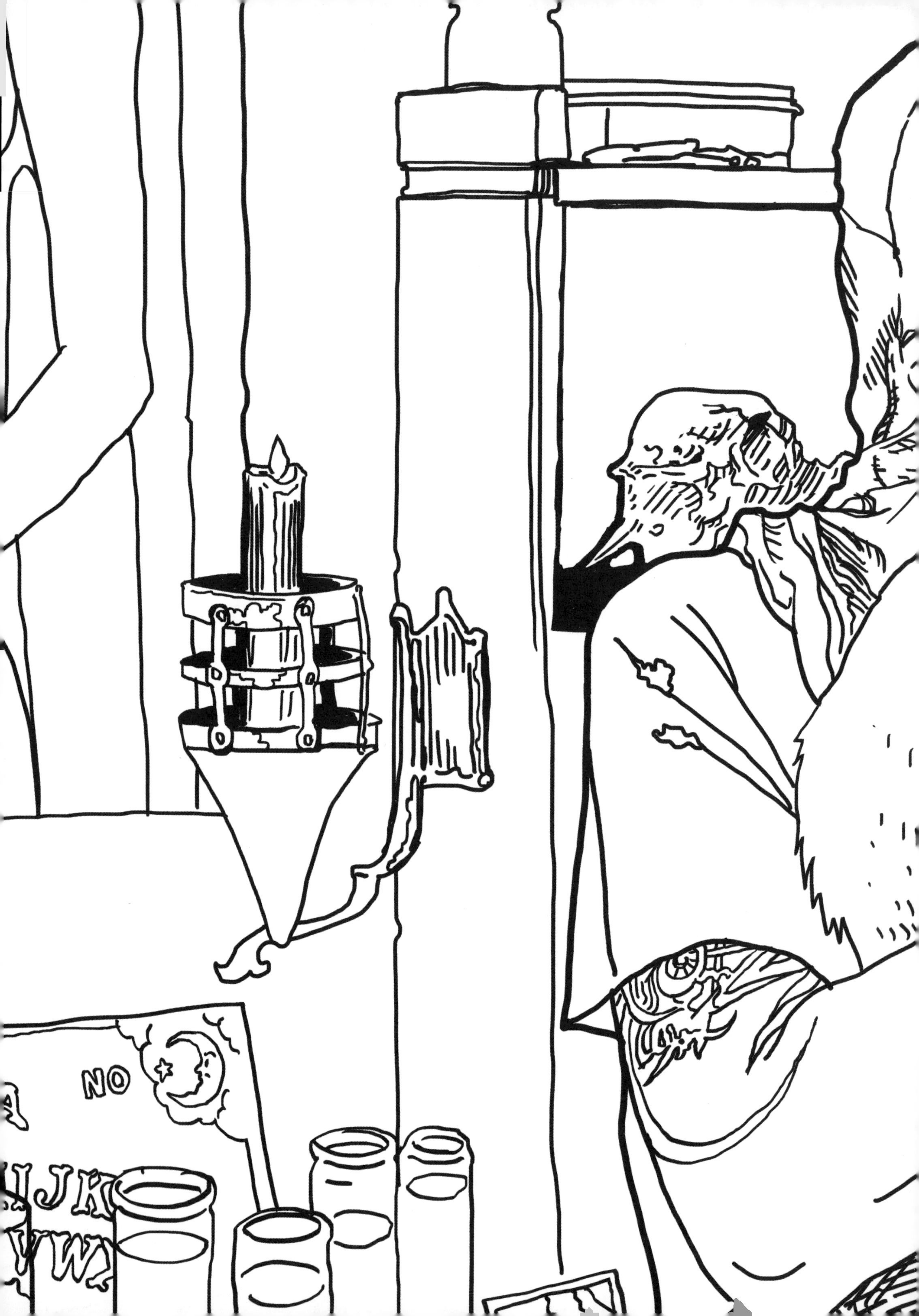
NO

THRASHER
CSS

TAINTED COCAINE, PART II
AND WE
The Stranger
The Stranger
The Stranger

LYMPI

FEEL THE FIRE